An
Anthony
Anthology

An
Anthony
Anthology

An ju

Rhapsody
61 Gainsborough Road, Felixstowe,
Suffolk IP11 7HS

ISBN 1 898030 26 X

Production copyright © 2003 **Judith Anthony**
www.author.co.uk/anju

British Library Cataloguing in Publication Data
available.

Cover photograph by Judith Anthony

Printed in Kent
by JRDigital Print Services Ltd
Rhapsody is an imprint of Author Publishing Ltd

For Matthew and James

Introduction

I have put together this anthology partly because the books where I first read and learned some of the poems are falling apart, and I wanted to have favourite poems in one place; and to give pleasure to my family and friends. The poems have been chosen because I have been fond of them for years; or because they strike a chord from the past for a place or a season; or because they resonate with my own feelings in their reflections on the big themes of life: and not least because I wanted to include some poems by little known and mostly unpublished poets, and friends.

The result is a collection ranging from the sixteenth century to the twenty first, reflecting on landscapes and love; living and dying; on war; and on the quirkiness of human beings, including poets. I hope it will bring pleasure to many, and am grateful to those who have a hand in editing, suggesting, and typing and especially to those who have written poems which are included.

Judith Anthony

2003

Poems

All Things Bright and Beautiful

All things bright and beautiful
All creatures great and small
All things wise and wonderful
The Lord God made them all.

Each little flower that opens
Each little bird that sings
He made their glowing colours
He made their tiny wings:

The purple-headed mountain
The river running by
The sunset and the morning,
That brightens up the sky:

All things bright and beautiful
All creatures great and small
All things wise and wonderful
The Lord God made them all.

Mrs Cecil Frances Alexander 1818-1895

Do Not Stand at my Grave and Weep

Do not stand at my grave and weep;
I am not there. I do not sleep.
I am a thousand winds that blow
I am the diamond glints on snow
I am the sunlight on ripened grain
I am the gentle autumn rain.
When you awaken in the morning's hush
I am the swift uplifting rush
Of quiet birds in circled flight.
I am the soft stars that shine at night.
Do not stand at my grave and cry;
I am not there. I did not die.

Anon

Indian Prayer

(traditional)

When I am dead
Cry for me a little
Think of me sometimes
But not too much.
Think of me now and again
As I was in life
At some moments it's pleasant to recall
But not for long.
Leave me in peace
And I shall leave you in peace
And while you live
Let your thoughts be with the living.

Anon

Lay Your Sleeping Head

Lay your sleeping head, my love,
Human on my faithless arm;
Time and fevers burn away
Individual beauty from
Thoughtful children, and the grave
Proves the child ephemeral:
But in my arms till break of day
Let the living creature lie,
Mortal, guilty, but to me
The entirely beautiful.

Soul and body have no bounds:
To lovers as they lie upon
Her tolerant enchanted slope
In their ordinary swoon,
Grave the vision Venus sends
Of supernatural sympathy,
Universal love and hope;
While an abstract insight wakes
Among the glaciers and the rocks
The hermit's sensual ecstasy.

Certainty, fidelity
On the stroke of midnight pass
Like vibrations of a bell
And fashionable madmen raise
Their pedantic boring cry:
Every farthing of the cost,
All the dreaded cards foretell,
Shall be paid, but from this night
Not a whisper, not a thought,
Not a kiss nor look be lost.

Beauty, midnight, vision dies:
Let the winds of dawn that blow
Softly round your dreaming head
Such a day of sweetness show
Eye and knocking heart may bless,
Find the mortal world enough;
Noons of dryness see you fed
By the involuntary powers,
Nights of insult let you pass
Watched by every human love.

W H Auden 1907-73

Look, Stranger

Look, stranger, at this island now
The leaping light for your delight discovers,
Stand stable here
And silent be,
That through the channels of the ear
May wander like a river
The swaying sound of the sea.
Here at the small field's ending pause
Where the chalk wall falls to the foam, and its tall ledges
Oppose the pluck
And knock of the tide,
And the shingle scrambles after the sucking surf,
and the gull lodges
A moment on its sheer side.

Far off like floating seeds the ships
Diverge on urgent voluntary errands:
And the full view
Indeed may enter
And move in memory as now these clouds do,
That pass the harbour mirror
And all the summer through the water saunter.

W H Auden

Night Mail

(Commentary for a G.P.O. Film)

I

This is the Night Mail crossing the Border,
Bringing the cheque and the postal order,

Letters for the rich, letters for the poor,
The shop at the corner, the girl next door.

Pulling up Beattock, a steady climb:
The gradient's against her, but she's on time.

Past cotton-grass and moorland boulder,
Shovelling white steam over her shoulder,

Snorting noisily, she passes
Silent miles of wind-bent grasses.

Birds turn their heads as she approaches,
Stare from bushes at her blank-faced coaches.

Sheep-dogs cannot turn her course;
They slumber on with paws across.

In the farm she passes no one wakes,
But a jug in a bedroom gently shakes.

II

Dawn freshens. Her climb is done.

Down towards Glasgow she descends,
Towards the steam tugs yelping down a glade of cranes,
Towards the fields of apparatus, the furnaces
Set on the dark plain like gigantic chessmen.
All Scotland waits for her:
In dark glens, beside pale-green lochs,
Men long for news.

III

Letters of thanks, letters from banks,
Letters of joy from girl and boy,
Receipted bills and invitations
To inspect new stock or to visit relations,
And applications for situations,
And timid lovers' declarations,
And gossip, gossip from all the nations,
News circumstantial, news financial,
Letters with holiday snaps to enlarge in,
Letter with faces scrawled on the margin,
Letters from uncles, cousins and aunts,
Letters to Scotland from the South of France,
Letters of condolence to Highlands and Lowlands,
Written on paper of every hue,
The pink, the violet, the white and the blue,
The chatty, the catty, the boring, the adoring,
The cold and official and the heart's outpouring,
Clever, stupid, short and long,
The typed and the printed and the spelt all wrong.

IV

Thousands are still asleep,
Dreaming of terrifying monsters
Or a friendly tea beside the band in Cranston's of Crawford's:
Asleep in working Glasgow, asleep in well-set Edinburgh,
Asleep in granite Aberdeen,
They continue their dreams,
But shall wake soon and hope for letters,
And none will hear the postman's knock
Without a quickening of the heart.
For who can bear to feel himself forgotten?

W H Auden

Beached Whale

(suggested by 'Paroles sur la Dune')

Victor Hugo
When the candle of his life guttered and burnt low
Walked bent along the shore.
Wondering how the loveliness of living
Could disappear across an endless moving sea
Into the vastness of the sky
And leave nothing.
Am I nothing more he asked
As his own dusk fell
Than a bitter gust of wind
Or a wave?
His only answer was
The laughing summer's day
And the blue sea holly at the water's edge
Le chardon bleu des sables.

I too look out across the dunes
My eye drawn along the waves' rim
To the distant shimmering sandspit that tongues
The bleached vapour where sea and sky
Fuse at the earth's edge
And like him consider
The transience of joy.
But in the unromantic age
And in the absence of blue sea holly
I am provided with an altogether more prosaic metaphor
A beached whale.
The fleshy oil grey mountain grossly erupts

From where plaited rivulets dredge
The calm expanse of the mudslicked bay.
Gulls wheel and scream
Their bead eyes vicious with greed in the leeward stink.
And a silent group of bystanders attempt perhaps to measure
The monstrous discrepancy between life and death.

Someone took photos of the whale
At successive stages of its long decomposition.
When they were juxtaposed across a wall
You saw the whale first fill the frame
Then in a flash become bone wreck
And shrink into nothing.
I would have liked the last snap
Of empty seascape
To feature a flower
Maybe a blue sea holly
Le chardon bleu des sables.

Angela Berger 1943 -

Lovers

The day I saw them on the beach
They were dancing and running hand in hand
Like children suddenly released,
The fresh spring sun filling their eyes
With delighted disbelief.
Around them the salt sharp wind tossed high
Spirals and pirouettes of larksong
In the washed air
And the allegretto duo of their voices
Wove scattered wove
Above the hushed suck and swell of the sea.
Then all at once their inner ecstasy
Spilled into the light
In a rush of irrepressible laughter
Whose streaming silver thread a skimming tern
Seized and carried low across the waves and out to sea.
Now gravely entwined
They set their forty something faces to the west
And walked on.
But I, colourless and quiet as the dunlins
Mirrored in the liquid sand was
Quite bereft of joy.

Angela Berger

Meditation on the A30

A man on his own in a car
  Is revenging himself on his wife;
He opens the throttle and bubbles with dottle
  And puffs at his pitiful life.

'She's losing her looks very fast,
  She loses her temper all day;
That lorry won't let me get past,
  This Mini is blocking my way.

'Why can't you step on it and shift her!
  I can't go on crawling like this!
At breakfast she said that she wished I was dead -
  Thank heavens we don't have to kiss.

'I'd like a nice blonde on my knee
  And one who won't argue or nag.
Who dares to come hooting at me?
  I only give way to a Jag.

'You're barmy or plastered, I'll pass you, you bastard -
  I will overtake you. I will!'
As he clenches his pipe, his moment is ripe
  And the corner's accepting its kill.

John Betjeman 1906 – 1984

Slough

Come, friendly bombs, and fall on Slough
It isn't fit for humans now,
There isn't grass to graze a cow
    Swarm over, Death!

Come, bombs, and blow to smithereens
Those air-conditioned, bright canteens,
Tinned fruit, tinned meat, tinned milk, tinned beans
    Tinned minds, tinned breath.

Mess up the mess they call a town -
A house for ninety-seven down
And once a week a half-a-crown
    For twenty years,

And get that man with double chin
Who'll always cheat and always win,
Who washes his repulsive skin
    In women's tears,

And smash his desk of polished oak
And smash his hands so used to stroke
And stop his boring dirty joke
    And make him yell.

But spare the bald young clerks who add
The profits of the stinking cad;
It's not their fault that they are mad,
　　They've tasted Hell.

It's not their fault they do not know
The birdsong from the radio,
It's not their fault they often go
　　To Maidenhead

And talk of sports and makes of cars
In various bogus Tudor bars
And daren't look up and see the stars
　　But belch instead.

In labour-saving homes, with care
Their wives frizz out peroxide hair
And dry it in synthetic air
　　And paint their nails.

Come, friendly bombs, and fall on Slough
To get it ready for the plough.
The cabbages are coming now;
　　The earth exhales.

John Betjeman

A Subaltern's Love-song

Miss J. Hunter Dunn, Miss J. Hunter Dunn,
Furnish'd and burnish'd by Aldershot sun,
What strenuous singles we played after tea,
We in the tournament – you against me!

Love-thirty, love-forty, oh! weakness of joy,
The speed of a swallow, the grace of a boy,
With carefullest carelessness, gaily you won,
I am weak from your loveliness, Joan Hunter Dunn.

Miss Joan Hunter Dunn, Miss Joan Hunter Dunn,
How mad I am, sad I am, glad that you won.
The warm-handled racket is back in its press,
But my shock-headed victor, she loves me no less.

Her father's euonymus shines as we walk,
And swing past the summer-house, buried in talk,
And cool the verandah that welcomes us in
To the six-o'clock news and a lime-juice and gin.

The scent of the conifers, sound of the bath,
The view from my bedroom of moss-dappled path,
As I struggle with double-end evening tie,
For we dance at the Golf Club, my victor and I.

On the floor of her bedroom lie blazer and shorts
And the cream-coloured walls are be-trophied with sports.
And westering, questioning settles the sun
On our low-leaded window, Miss Joan Hunter Dunn.

The Hillman is waiting, the light's in the hall,
The pictures of Egypt are bright on the wall,
My sweet, I am standing beside the oak stair
And there on the landing's the light on your hair.

By roads "not adopted ", by woodlanded ways,
She drove to the club in the late summer haze,
Into nine-o'clock Camberley, heavy with bells
And mushroomy, pine-woody, evergreen smells.

Miss Joan Hunter Dunn, Miss Joan Hunter Dunn,
I can hear from the car-park the dance has begun.
Oh! full Surrey twilight! importunate band!
Oh! strongly adorable tennis-girl's hand!

Around us are Rovers and Austins afar,
Above us, the intimate roof of the car,
And here on my right is the girl of my choice,
With the tilt of her nose and the chime of her voice

And the scent of her wrap, and the words never said,
And the ominous, ominous dancing ahead.
We sat in the car park till twenty to one
And now I'm engaged to Miss Joan Hunter Dunn.

John Betjeman

Trebetherick

We used to picnic where the thrift
Grew deep and tufted to the edge;
We saw the yellow foam-flakes drift
In trembling sponges on the ledge
Below us, till the wind would lift
Them up the cliff and o'er the hedge.
Sand in the sandwiches, wasps in the tea,
Sun on our bathing-dresses heavy with the wet,
Squelch of the bladder-wrack waiting for the sea,
Fleas round the tamarisk, an early cigarette.

From where the coastguard houses stood
One used to see, below the hill,
The lichened branches of a wood
In summer silver-cool and still;
And there the Shade of Evil could
Stretch out at us from Shilla Mill.
Thick with sloe and blackberry, uneven in the light,
Lonely ran the hedge, the heavy meadow was remote,
The oldest part of Cornwall was the wood as black as night,
And the pheasant and the rabbit lay torn open at the throat.

But when a storm was at its height,
And feathery slate was black in rain,
And tamarisks were hung with light
And golden sand was brown again,
Spring tide and blizzard would unite
And sea came flooding up the lane.

Waves full of treasure then were roaring up the beach,
Ropes round our mackintoshes, waders warm and dry,
We waited for the wreckage to come swirling into reach,
Ralph, Vasey, Alastair, Biddy, John and I.

Then roller into roller curled
And thundered down the rocky bay,
And we were in a water-world
Of rain and blizzard, sea and spray,
And one against the other hurled
We struggled round to Greenaway.

Blessèd be St. Enodoc, blessèd be the wave,
Blessèd be the springy turf, we pray, pray to thee,
Ask for our children all the happy days you gave
To Ralph, Vasey, Alastair, Biddy, John and me.

John Betjeman

Harrow-on-the-Hill

When melancholy Autumn comes to Wembley
And electric trains are lighted after tea
The poplars near the Stadium are trembly
With their tap and tap and whispering to me,
Like the sound of little breakers
Spreading out along the surf-line
When the estuary's filling
With the sea.

Then Harrow-on-the-Hill's a rocky island
And Harrow churchyard full of sailors' graves
And the constant click and kissing of the trolley buses
hissing
Is the level to the Wealdstone turned to waves
And the rumble of the railway
Is the thunder of the rollers
As they gather up for plunging
Into caves.

There's a storm cloud to the westward over Kenton,
There's a line of harbour lights at Perivale,
Is it rounding rough Pentire in a flood of sunset fire
The little fleet of trawlers under sail?
Can those boats be only roof tops
As they stream along the skyline
In a race for port and Padstow
With the gale?

John Betjeman

from The Burning of Leaves

Now is the time for the burning of the leaves.
They go to the fire; the nostril pricks with smoke
Wandering slowly into a weeping mist.
Brittle and blotched, ragged and rotten sheaves!
A flame seizes the smouldering ruin and bites
On stubborn stalks that crackle as they resist.

The last hollyhock's fallen tower is dust:
All the spices of June are a bitter reek,
All the extravagant riches spent and mean.
All burns! The reddest rose is a ghost;
Sparks whirl up, to expire in the mist: the wild
Fingers of fire are making corruption clean.

Now is the time for stripping the spirit bare,
Time for the burning of days ended and done,
Idle solace of things that have gone before,
Rootless hope and fruitless desire are there:
Let them go to the fire with never a look behind.
The world that was ours is a world that is ours no more.

They will come again, the leaf and the flower, to arise
From squalor of rottenness into the old splendour,
And magical scents to a wondering memory bring:
The same glory, to shine upon different eyes.
Earth cares for her own ruins, naught for ours.
Nothing is certain, only the certain spring.

Laurence Binyon 1869 – 1943

The Clod and the Pebble

Love seeketh not Itself to please,
Nor for itself hath any care,
But for another gives its ease,
And builds a Heaven in Hell's despair.'

So sung a little Clod of Clay
Trodden with the cattle's feet,
But a Pebble of the brook
Warbled out these metres meet:

Love seeketh only Self to please,
To bind another to Its delight,
Joys in another's loss of ease,
And builds a Hell in Heaven's despite.'

William Blake 1757 – 1827

The Sick Rose

O Rose, thou art sick!
The invisible worm
That flies in the night,
In the howling storm,

Has found out thy bed
Of crimson joy,
And his dark secret love
Does thy life destroy.

William Blake

The Tyger

Tyger! Tyger! burning bright
In the forests of the night,
What immortal hand or eye
Could frame thy fearful symmetry?

In what distant deeps or skies
Burnt the fire of thine eyes?
On what wings dare he aspire?
What the hand dare seize the fire?

And what shoulder, and what art,
Could twist the sinews of thy heart?
And when thy heart began to beat,
What dread hand? and what dread feet?

What the hammer? What the chain?
In what furnace was thy brain?
What the anvil? what dread grasp
Dare its deadly terrors clasp?

When the stars threw down their spears,
And water'd heaven with their tears,
Did he smile his work to see?
Did he who made the Lamb make thee?

Tyger! Tyger! burning bright
In the forests of the night,
What immortal hand or eye
Dare frame thy fearful symmetry?

William Blake

The Soldier

If I should die, think only this of me:
That there's some corner of a foreign field
That is for ever England. There shall be
In that rich earth a richer dust concealed;
A dust whom England bore, shaped, made aware,
Gave, once, her flowers to love, her ways to roam,
A body of England's, breathing English air,
Washed by the rivers, blest by suns of home.
And think, this heart, all evil shed away,
A pulse in the eternal mind, no less
Gives somewhere back the thoughts by England given;
Her sights and sounds; dreams happy as her day;
And laughter, learnt of friends; and gentleness,
In hearts at peace, under an English heaven.

Rupert Brooke 1887 – 1915

The Old Vicarage, Grantchester

(Café des Westens, Berlin, May 1912)

Just now the lilac is in bloom,
All before my little room;
And in my flower-beds, I think,
Smile the carnation and the pink;
And down the borders, well I know,
The poppy and the pansy blow …
Oh! there the chestnuts, summer through,
Beside the river make for you
A tunnel of green gloom, and sleep
Deeply above; and green and deep
The stream mysterious glides beneath,
Green as a dream and deep as death.
- Oh, damn! I know it! and I know
How the May fields all golden show,
And when the day is young and sweet,
Gild gloriously the bare feet.
That run to bathe …
                    Du lieber Gott!

Here am I, sweating, sick, and hot,
And there the shadowed waters fresh
Lean up to embrace the naked flesh.
Temperamentvoll German Jews
Drink beer around; - and *there* the dews
Are soft beneath a morn of gold.
Here tulips bloom as they are told;
Unkempt about those hedges blows
An English unofficial rose;
And there the unregulated sun
Slopes down to rest when day is done,

And wakes a vague unpunctual star,
A slippered Hesper; and there are
Meads towards Haslingfield and Coton
Where *das Betreten's* not *verboten*.

εἰθε γευοιμην ... would I were
In Grantchester, in Grantchester!
Some, it may be, can get in touch
With Nature there, or Earth, or such.
And clever modern men have seen
A Faun a-peeping through the green,
And felt the Classics were not dead,
To glimpse a Naiad's reedy head,
Or hear the Goat-foot piping low:...
But these are things I do not know.
I only know that you may lie
Day-long and watch the Cambridge sky,
And, flower-lulled in sleepy grass,
Hear the cool lapse of hours pass,
Until the centuries blend and blur
In Grantchester, in Grantchester ...
Still in the dawnlit waters cool
His ghostly Lordship swims his pool,
And tries the strokes, essays the tricks,
Long learnt on Hellespont, of Styx.
Dan Chaucer hears his river still
Chatter beneath a phantom mill.

Tennyson notes, with studious eye,
How Cambridge waters hurry by ...
And in that garden, black and white,
Creep whispers through the grass all night;
And spectral dance, before the dawn,

27

A hundred Vicars down the lawn;
Curates, long dust, will come and go
On lissom, clerical, printless toe;
And oft between the boughs is seen
The sly shade of a Rural Dean ...
Till, at a shiver in the skies,
Vanishing with Satanic cries,
The prim ecclesiastic rout
Leaves but a startled sleeper-out,
Grey heavens, the first bird's drowsy calls,
The falling house that never falls.

God! I will pack, and take a train,
And get me to England once again!
For England's the one land, I know,
Where men with Splendid Hearts may go;
And Cambridgeshire, of all England,
The shire for Men who Understand;
And of *that* district I prefer
The lovely hamlet Grantchester.
For Cambridge people rarely smile,
Being urban, squat, and packed with guile;
And Royston men in the far South
Are black and fierce and strange of mouth;
At Over they fling oaths at one,
And worse than oaths at Trumpington,
And Ditton girls are mean and dirty,
And there's none in Harston under thirty,
And folks in Shelford and those parts
Have twisted lips and twisted hearts,
And Barton men make Cockney rhymes,
And Coton's full of nameless crimes,
And things are done you'd not believe

At Madingley, on Christmas Eve.
Strong men have run for miles and miles,
When one from Cherry Hinton smiles;
Strong men have blanched, and shot their wives,
Rather than send them to St Ives;
Strong men have cried like babes, bydam,
To hear what happened at Babraham.
But Grantchester! ah, Grantchester!
There's peace and holy quiet there,
Great clouds along pacific skies,
And men and women with straight eyes,
Lithe children lovelier than a dream,
A bosky wood, a slumbrous stream,
And little kindly winds that creep
Round twilight corners, half asleep.
In Grantchester their skins are white;
They bathe by day, they bathe by night;
The women there do all they ought;
The men observe the Rules of Thought.
They love the Good; they worship Truth;
They laugh uproariously in youth;
(And when they get to feeling old,
They up and shoot themselves, I'm told) …

Ah God! to see the branches stir
Across the moon at Grantchester!
To smell the thrilling-sweet and rotten
Unforgettable, unforgotten
River-smell, and hear the breeze
Sobbing in the little trees.
Say, do the elm-clumps greatly stand
Still guardians of that holy land?
The chestnuts shade, in reverend dream,

The yet unacademic stream?
Is dawn a secret shy and cold
Anadyomene, silver-gold?
And sunset still a golden sea
From Haslingfield to Madingley?
And after, ere the night is born,
Do hares come out about the corn?
Oh, is the water sweet and cool,
Gentle and brown, above the pool?
And laughs the immortal river still
Under the mill, under the mill?
Say, is there Beauty yet to find?
And Certainty? and Quiet kind?
Deep meadows yet, for to forget
The lies, and truths, and pain? ... oh! yet
Stands the Church clock at ten to three?
And is there honey still for tea?

Rupert Brooke

Home-thoughts, from Abroad

Oh, to be in England
Now that April's there,
And whoever wakes in England
Sees, some morning, unaware,
That the lowest boughs and the brushwood sheaf
Round the elm-tree bole are in tiny leaf,
While the chaffinch sings on the orchard bough
In England – now!

And after April, when May follows,
And the whitethroat builds, and all the swallows -
Hark! where my blossomed pear-tree in the hedge
Leans to the field and scatters on the clover
Blossoms and dewdrops – at the bent spray's edge –
That's the wise thrush; he sings each song twice over,
Lest you should think he never could recapture
The first fine careless rapture!
And though the fields look rough with hoary dew,
All will be gay when noontide wakes anew
The buttercups, the little children's dower,
- Far brighter than this gaudy melon-flower!

Robert Browning 1812 - 1889

My Last Duchess

That's my last Duchess painted on the wall,
Looking as if she were alive. I call
That piece a wonder, now: Frà Pandolf's hands
Worked busily a day, and there she stands.
Will't please you sit and look at her? I said
'Frà Pandolf' by design, for never read
Strangers like you that pictured countenance,
The depth and passion of its earnest glance,
But to myself they turned, (since none puts by
The curtain I have drawn for you, but I)
And seemed as they would ask me, if they durst,
How such a glance came there; so, not the first
Are you to turn and ask thus. Sir, 'twas not
Her husband's presence only, called that spot
Of joy into the Duchess' cheek: perhaps
Frà Pandolf chanced to say 'Her mantle laps
Over my lady's wrist too much,' or 'Paint
Must never hope to reproduce the faint
Half-flush that dies along her throat:' such stuff
Was courtesy, she thought, and cause enough
For calling up that spot of joy. She had
A heart – how shall I say? – too soon made glad,
Too easily impressed; she liked whate'er
She looked on, and her looks went everywhere.
Sir, 'twas all one! My favour at her breast,
The dropping of the daylight in the West,
The bough of cherries some officious fool
Broke in the orchard for her, the white mule
She rode with round the terrace – all and each

Would draw from her alike the approving speech,
Or blush, at least. She thanked men, - good! But thanked
Somehow – I know not how – as if she ranked
My gift of a nine-hundred-years-old name
With anybody's gift. Who'd stoop to blame
This sort of trifling? Even had you skill
In speech – (which I have not) – to make your will
Quite clear to such an one, and say, 'Just this
Or that in you disgusts me; here you miss,
Or there exceed the mark' – and if she let
Herself be lessoned so, nor plainly set
Her wits to yours, forsooth, and made excuse,
- E'en then would be some stooping; and I choose
Never to stoop. Oh, sir, she smiled, no doubt,
Whene'er I passed her; but who passed without
Much the same smile? This grew; I gave commands;
Then all smiles stopped together. There she stands
As if alive. Will't please you rise? We'll meet
The company below, then. I repeat,
The Count your master's known munificence
Is ample warrant that no just pretence
Of mine for dowry will be disallowed;
Though his fair daughter's self, as I avowed
At starting, is my object. Nay, we'll go
Together down, sir. Notice Neptune, though,
Taming a sea-horse, thought a rarity,
Which Claus of Innsbruck cast in bronze for me!

Robert Browning

All's Right with the World

The year's at the spring,
And day's at the morn;
Morning's at seven;
The hill-side's dew-pearled;
The lark's on the wing;
The snail's on the thorn:
God's in his heaven –
All's right with the world!

Robert Browning

Wörther See

Would that wars might end for all soldiers like this:
Swimming, rowing, sailing, deep walks in the woods;
Landscapes rich in vines and maize, flowers and fruit;
Natives clean and honest, plump, wooable girls;
Food well-cooked and varied, camp discipline light;
No more danger, boredom, dirt, weariness, din;
Pride in battles won, the world's gratitude earned;
Ease in which to stretch the cramped limbs of the soul:
Would that wars might end for all soldiers like this.

Norman Cameron 1905 – 1953

Jabberwocky

'Twas brillig, and the slithy toves
Did gyre and gimble in the wabe;
All mimsy were the borogoves,
And the mome raths outgrabe.

'Beware the Jabberwock, my son!
The jaws that bite, the claws that catch!
Beware the Jubjub bird, and shun
The frumious Bandersnatch!'

He took his vorpal sword in hand:
Long time the manxome foe he sought –
So rested he by the Tumtum tree,
And stood awhile in thought.

And as in uffish thought he stood,
The Jabberwock, with eyes of flame,
Came whiffling through the tulgey wood,
And burbled as it came!

One, two! One, two! And through and through
The vorpal blade went snicker-snack!
He left it dead, and with its head
He went galumphing back.

'And hast thou slain the Jabberwock?
Come to my arms, my beamish boy!
O frabjous day! Callooh! Callay!'
He chortled in his joy.

'Twas brillig, and the slithy toves
Did gyre and gimble in the wabe;
All mimsy were the borogoves,
And the mome raths outgrabe.

Lewis Carroll 1832 - 1898

Wine and Water

Old Noah he had an ostrich farm and fowls on the largest scale,
He ate his egg with a ladle in an egg-cup big as a pail,
And the soup he took was an Elephant Soup and the fish he took
was Whale,
But they all were small to the cellar he took when he set out to sail,
And Noah he often said to his wife when he sat down to dine,
'I don't care where the water goes if it doesn't get into the wine.'

The cataract of the cliff of heaven fell blinding off the brink
As if it would wash the stars away as suds go down a sink,
The seven heavens came roaring down for the throats of hell to
drink,
And Noah he cocked his eye and said, 'It looks like rain, I think,
The water has drowned the Matterhorn as deep as a Mendip mine,
But I don't care where the water goes if it doesn't get into the wine.'

But Noah he sinned, as we have sinned; on tipsy feet we trod,
Till a great big black teetotaler was sent to us for a rod,
And you can't get wine at a P.S.A., or chapel, or Eisteddfod,
For the Curse of Water has come again because of the wrath of God,
And water is on the Bishop's board and the Higher Thinker's shrine,
But I don't care where the water goes if it doesn't get into the wine.

G K Chesterton 1874-1936

Morning

The morning comes, the drops of dew
Hang on the grass and bushes too;
The sheep more eager bite the grass
Whose moisture gleams like drops of glass;
The heifer licks in grass and dew
That make her drink and fodder too.
The little bird his morn-song gives,
His breast wet with the dripping leaves,
Then stops abruptly just to fly
And catch the wakened butterfly,
That goes to sleep behind the flowers
Or backs of leaves from dews and showers.
The yellow-hammer, haply blest,
Sits by the dyke upon her nest;
The long grass hides her from the day,
The water keeps the boys away.
The morning sun is round and red
As crimson curtains round a bed,
The dewdrops hang on barley horns
As beads the necklace thread adorns,
The dewdrops hang wheat-ears upon
Like golden drops against the sun.
Hedge-sparrows in the bush cry 'tweet',
O'er nests larks winnow in the wheat,
Till the sun turns gold and gets more high,
And paths are clean and grass gets dry,
And longest shadows pass away.
And brightness is the blaze of day.

John Clare 1793 – 1864

40

Arabia

Far are the shades of Arabia,
Where the Princes ride at noon,
'Mid the verdurous vales and thickets,
Under the ghost of the moon;
And so dark is that vaulted purple
Flowers in the forest rise
And toss into blossom 'gainst the phantom stars
Pale in the noonday skies.

Sweet is the music of Arabia
In my heart, when out of dreams
I still in the thin clear mirk of dawn
Descry her gliding streams;
Hear her strange lutes on the green banks
Ring loud with the grief and delight
Of the dim-silked, dark-haired Musicians
In the brooding silence of night.

They haunt me - her lutes and her forests;
No beauty on earth I see
But shadowed with that dream recalls
Her loveliness to me:
Still eyes look coldly upon me,
Cold voices whisper and say -
'He is crazed with the spell of far Arabia,
They have stolen his wits away.'

Walter de la Mare 1873 - 1956

Trees

Of all the trees in England,
Her sweet three corners in,
Only the Ash, the bonnie Ash
Burns fierce while it is green.

Of all the trees in England,
From sea to sea again,
The Willow loveliest stoops her boughs
Beneath the driving rain.

Of all the trees in England,
Past frankincense and myrrh,
There's none for smell, of bloom and smoke,
Like Lime and Juniper.

Of all the trees in England,
Oak, Elder, Elm and Thorn,
The Yew alone burns lamps of peace
For them that lie forlorn.

Walter de la Mare

Untitled

A wet sheet and a flowing sea,
A wind that follows fast
And fills the white and rustling sail
And bends the gallant mast;
And bends the gallant mast, my boys,
While like the eagle free
Away the good ship flies and leaves
Old England on the lee.

O for a soft and gentle wind!
I heard a fair one cry;
But give to me the snoring breeze
And white waves heaving high;
And white waves heaving high, my lads,
The good ship tight and free –
The world of waters is our home,
And merry men are we.

There's tempest in yon hornéd moon,
And lightning in yon cloud;
But hark the music, mariners!
The wind is piping loud;
The wind is piping loud, my boys,
The lightning flashes free –
While the hollow oak our palace is,
Our heritage the sea

Allan Cunningham 1784 – 1842

Song

Sweetest love, I do not goe,
For weariness of thee,
Nor in hope the world can show
A fitter Love for mee;
But since that I
Must dye at last, 'tis best,
To use my selfe in jest
Thus by fain'd deaths to dye;

Yesternight the Sunne went hence,
And yet is here to day,
He hath no desire nor sense,
Nor halfe so short a way:
Then feare not mee,
But believe that I shall make
Speedier journeys, since I take
More wings and spurres than hee.

O how feeble is man's power,
That if good fortune fall,
Cannot adde another houre,
Nor a lost houre recall!
But come bad chance,
And wee joyne to' it our strength,
And wee teach it art and length,
It selfe o'r us to' advance.

When thou sigh'st, thou sigh'st not winde,
But sigh'st my soule away,
When thou weep'st, unkindly kinde,
My lifes blood doth decay.
It cannot bee
That thou lov'st mee, as thou say'st,
If in thine my life thou waste,
That art the best of mee.

Let not thy divining heart
Forethinke me any ill,
Destiny may take thy part,
And may thy feares fulfill;
But thinke that wee
Are but turn'd aside to sleepe;
They who one another keepe
Alive, ne'r parted bee.

John Donne 1572 – 1631

Cairo Jag

Shall I get drunk or cut myself a piece of cake,
a pasty Syrian with a few words of English
or the Turk who says she is a princess – she dances
apparently by levitation? Or Marcelle, Parisienne
always preoccupied with her dull dead lover:
she has all the photographs and his letters
tied in a bundle and stamped *Décedé* in mauve ink.
All this takes place in a stink of jasmine,

But there are the streets dedicated to sleep
stenches and the sour smells, the sour cries
do not disturb their application to slumber
all day, scattered on the pavement like rags
afflicted with fatalism and hashish. The women
offering their children brown-paper breasts
dry and twisted, elongated like the skull,
Holbein's signature. But this stained white town
is something in accordance with mundane conventions –
Marcelle drops her Gallic airs and tragedy
suddenly shrieks in Arabic about the fare
with the cabman, links herself so
with the somnambulists and legless beggars:
it is all one, all as you have heard.

But by a day's travelling you reach a new world
the vegetation is of iron
dead tanks, gun barrels split like celery
the metal brambles have no flowers or berries
and there are all sorts of manure, you can imagine
the dead themselves, their boots, clothes and possessions
clinging to the ground, a man with no head
has a packet of chocolate and a souvenir of Tripoli.

Keith Douglas 1920 – 1944

The Naming of Cats

The Naming of Cats is a difficult matter,
It isn't just one of your holiday games;
You may think at first I'm as mad as a hatter
When I tell you, a cat must have
THREE DIFFERENT NAMES.
First of all, there's the name that the family use daily,
Such as Peter, Augustus, Alonzo or James,
Such as Victor or Jonathan, George or Bill Bailey –
All of them sensible everyday names.
There are fancier names if you think they sound sweeter,
Some for the gentlemen, some for the dames:
Such as Plato, Admetus, Electra, Demeter –
But all of them sensible everyday names.
But I tell you, a cat needs a name that's particular,
A name that's peculiar, and more dignified,
Else how can he keep up his tail perpendicular,
Or spread out his whiskers, or cherish his pride?
Of names of this kind, I can give you a quorum,
Such at Munkustrap, Quaxo, Coricopat,
Such as Bombalurina, or else Jellylorum –
Names that never belong to more than one cat.
But above and beyond there's still one name left over,
And that is the name that you never will guess;
The name that no human research can discover –

But THE CAT HIMSELF KNOWS, and will never confess.
When you notice a cat in profound meditation,
The reason, I tell you, is always the same:
His mind is engaged in a rapt contemplation
Of the thought, of the thought, of the thought of his name:
His ineffable effable
Effanineffable
Deep and inscrutable singular Name.

T S Eliot

East Coker from the 'Four Quartets'

I

In my beginning is my end. In succession
Houses rise and fall, crumble, are extended,
Are removed, destroyed, restored, or in their place
Is an open field, or a factory, or a by-pass.
Old stone to new building, old timber to new fires,
Old fires to ashes, and ashes to the earth
Which is already flesh, fur and faeces,
Bone of man and beast, cornstalk and leaf.
Houses live and die: there is a time for building
And a time for living and for generation
And a time for the wind to break the loosened pane
And to shake the wainscot where the field-mouse trots
And to shake the tattered arras woven with a silent motto.

In my beginning is my end. Now the light falls
Across the open field, leaving the deep lane
Shuttered with branches, dark in the afternoon,
Where you lean against a bank while a van passes,
And the deep lane insists on the direction
Into the village, in the electric heat
Hypnotised. In a warm haze the sultry light
Is absorbed, not refracted, by grey stone.
The dahlias sleep in the empty silence.
Wait for the early owl
In that open field
If you do not come too close, if you do not come too close,
On a summer midnight, you can hear the music

Of the weak pipe and the little drum
And see them dancing around the bonfire
The association of man and woman
In daunsinge, signifying matrimonie –
A dignified and commodious sacrament.
Two and two, necessarye coniunction,
Holding eche other by the hand or the arm
Whiche betokeneth concorde. Round and round the fire
Leaping through the flames, or joined in circles,
Rustically-solemn or in rustic laughter
Lifting heavy feet in clumsy shoes,
Earth feet, loam feet, lifted in country mirth
Mirth of those long since under earth
Nourishing the corn, Keeping time,
Keeping the rhythm in their dancing
As in their living in the living seasons
The time of the seasons and the constellations
The time of milking and the time of harvest
The time of the coupling of man and woman
And that of beasts. Feet rising and falling.
Eating and drinking. Dung and death.

Dawn points, and another day
Prepares for heat and silence. Out at sea the dawn wind
Wrinkles and slides. I am here
Or there, or elsewhere. In my beginning.

II

What is the late November doing
With the disturbance of the spring
And creatures of the summer heat,
And snowdrops writhing under feet.
And hollyhocks that aim too high
Red into grey and tumble down
Late roses filled with early snow?
Thunder rolled by the rolling stars
Simulates triumphal cars
Deployed in constellated wars
Scorpion fights against the Sun
Until the Sun and Moon go down
Comets weep and Leonids fly
Hunt the heavens and the plains
Whirled in a vortex that shall bring
The world to that destructive fire
Which burns before the ice-cap reigns.

That was a way of putting it – not very satisfactory:
A periphrastic study in a worn-out poetical fashion,
Leaving one still with the intolerable wrestle
With words and meanings. The poetry does not matter.
It was not (to start again) what one had expected.
What was to be the value of the long looked forward to,
Long hoped for calm, the autumnal serenity
And the wisdom of age? Had they deceived us
Or deceived themselves, the quiet-voiced elders,
Bequeathing us merely a receipt for deceit?
The serenity only a deliberate hebetude,
The wisdom only the knowledge of dead secrets
Useless in the darkness into which they peered

Or from which they turned their eyes.
There is, it seems to us,
At best, only a limited value
In the knowledge derived from experience.
The knowledge imposes a pattern, and falsifies,
For the pattern is new in every moment
And every moment is a new and shocking
Valuation of all we have been. We are only undeceived
Of that which, deceiving, could no longer harm.
In the middle, not only in the middle of the way
But all the way, in a dark wood, in a bramble,
On the edge of a grimpen,
where there is no secure foothold,
And menaced by monsters, fancy lights,
Risking enchantment. Do not let me hear
Of the wisdom of old men, but rather of their folly,
Their fear of fear and frenzy, their fear of possession
Of belonging to another, or to others, or to God.
The only wisdom we can hope to acquire.
Is the wisdom of humility: humility is endless.

The houses are all gone under the sea.

The dancers are all gone under the hill.

III

O dark dark dark. They all go into the dark,
The vacant interstellar spaces, the vacant into the vacant,
The captains, merchant bankers, eminent men of letters,
The generous patrons of art, the statesmen and the rulers,
Distinguished civil servants, chairmen of many committees,
Industrial lords and petty contractors, all go into the dark,
And dark the Sun and Moon, and the Almanach de Gotha
And the Stock Exchange Gazette, the Directory of Directors,
And cold the sense and lost the motive of action.
And we all go with them, into the silent funeral,
Nobody's funeral, for there is no one to bury.
I said to my soul, be still, and let the dark come upon you
Which shall be the darkness of god. As, in a theatre,
The lights are extinguished, for the scene to be changed
With a hollow rumble of wings, with a movement of
darkness on darkness,
And we know that the hills and the trees,
the distant panorama
And the bold imposing façade are all being rolled away -
Or as, when an underground train, in the tube,
stops too long between stations
And the conversation rises and slowly fades into silence
And you see behind every face
the mental emptiness deepen
Leaving only the growing terror of nothing to think about;
Or when, under ether, the mind is conscious
but conscious of nothing -
I said to my soul, be still, and wait without hope
For hope would be hope for the wrong thing,
wait without love.
For love would be love of the wrong thing; there is yet faith

But the faith and the love
and the hope are all in the waiting.
Wait without thought, for you are not ready for
thought:
So the darkness shall be the light,
and the stillness the dancing.
Whisper of running streams, and the winter lightning.
The wild thyme unseen and the wild strawberry,
The laughter in the garden, echoed ecstasy
Not lost, but requiring, pointing to the agony
Of death and birth.
You say I am repeating
Something I have said before. I shall say it again.
Shall I say it again? In order to arrive there,
To arrive where you are, to get from where you are not,
You must go by a way wherein there is no ecstasy.
In order to arrive at what you do not know
You must go by a way which is the way of ignorance.
In order to possess what you do not possess
You must go by the way of dispossession.
In order to arrive at what you are not
You must go through the way in which you are not.
And what you own is what you do not own
And where you are is where you are not.

IV

The wounded surgeon plies the steel
That questions the distempered part;
Beneath the bleeding hands we feel
The sharp compassion of the healer's art.
Resolving the enigma of the fever chart.

Our only health is the disease
If we obey the dying nurse
Whose constant care is not to please
But to remind of our, and Adam's curse,
And that, to be restored, our sickness must grow worse.
The whole earth is our hospital
Endowed by the ruined millionaire,
Wherein, if we do well, we shall
Die of the absolute paternal care
That will not leave us, but prevents us everywhere.

The chill ascends from feet to knees,
The fever sings in mental wires.
If to be warmed, then I must freeze
And quake in frigid purgatorial fires
Of which the flame is roses, and the smoke is briars.

The dripping blood our only drink,
The bloody flesh our only food:
In spite of which we like to think
That we are sound, substantial flesh and blood -
Again, in spite of that, we call this Friday good.

V

So here I am, in the middle way,
having had twenty years -
Twenty years largely wasted,
the years of *l'entre deux guerres* -

Trying to learn to use words, and every attempt
Is a wholly new start, and a different kind of failure
Because one has only learnt to get the better of words
For the thing one no longer has to say, or the way in
which
One is no longer disposed to say it.
And so each venture
Is a new beginning, a raid on the inarticulate
With shabby equipment always deteriorating
In the general mess of imprecision of feeling,
Undisciplined squads of emotion.
And what there is to conquer
By strength and submission, has already been
discovered
Once or twice, or several times,
by men whom one cannot hope
To emulate - but there is no competition -
There is only the fight to recover what has been lost
And found and lost again and again:
and now, under conditions
That seem unpropitious.
But perhaps neither gain nor loss.
For us, there is only the trying.
The rest is not our business.

Home is where one starts from. As we grow older
The world becomes stranger,
the pattern more complicated
Of dead and living. Not the intense moment
Isolated, with no before and after,

But a lifetime burning in every moment
And not the lifetime of one man only
But of old stones that cannot be deciphered.
There is a time for the evening under starlight,
A time for the evening under lamplight
(The evening with the photograph album).
Love is most nearly itself
When here and now cease to matter.
Old men ought to be explorers
Here and there does not matter
We must be still and still moving
Into another intensity
For a further union, a deeper communion
Through the dark cold and the empty desolation,
The wave cry, the wind cry, the vast waters
Of the petrel and the porpoise.
In my end is my beginning.

T S Eliot

A fine place

Low tide, baring the rocky path
to the Worm.
Leaping or scrambling we arrive

At the bridge between the humps
we choose
to scatter his ashes

Ashes blowing back
as well as down
final flurries
Memories swirl, flying

And later we give the rest
of the ashes to the rock-pools
by a flowing stream

Home along the high cliffs
we silently remember
times past

Afterwards the flights
over Overton Mere
and the Worm
High moments to recall

The bridge has a name,
Devil's Bridge, no matter:
It is a fine place to celebrate his life.

Judith Elton 1945 -

Anglian Marshes, thoughts on a train

High skies
Thin delicate horizons telling
The specific place
Wide skies
Limpid wash on Whatman rough

Hazy names, Sea Palling, Horsey,
Somerleyton, Thurne
Kalima and days afloat
Sailing, gaff-rigged with wooden boom
Allowed to haul the sheets and
Leap to anchor in the reed beds
Thermos flasks and Grandpa

Windy beaches and stinging marram grass
Au pairs and spaghetti
Thirty years on
Southwold, and my own children
Icecream and fish
Ten years later a wedding
At the pub

Snape's resonance
A boy's plaintive cry
The Little Sweep and swooping
Human chorus of birds
Bearded Birtwhistle
Interval oysters
Balcony chat and lonely
Marshes presiding, whispering.

Blakeney, Holkham and Wells
Warm mist hanging over a
Molten grey sea
Sand sea's edge and sky sea join
As one

Blythburgh's great tower
Floodlit
Evensong with trumpets
And viols
Angels watch and listen
Above.

Beccles, Bungay and boats
And the road home
Waveney, Fressingfield and
Friends long gone

Reeded foregrounds to apple green marshes
Grey green treelines and
Stippled shingle beaches with
White crested seas

Watercolour memories
In their frames.

Judith Elton

Cloona Walks

1: Brackloon Wood

Birches stand solitary as sentinels,
or grouped like lanky lads loitering
Ancient oaks tower above lesser trees
Lichens pale sage, crinkled, cling to branches
Bright green rugs of moss
lie on fallen trees

Small streams splash and scurry
to join the Owenwee
tumbling and racing
Crystal raindrops hang like jewels
on every twig

The wood is friendly – an essential
wood for all time.

2: Bartraw Strand

Curlew above my head, curlew cry
Aquamarine sea and scudding whichever way clouds
The wind bowls the silver marram grasses over
And Croagh Patrick stands crow dark behind

Lush lime green grass
Black horned sheep, curious.
Stony shores and, near but far,
Clew Bay's deserted isles.
Redshanks swoop and whoop
At the rising tide.

Judith Elton

Not in my name

Not in my name
The click of the canopy
The precision minds
Trained and briefed
The planes loaded with weapons
Designed to destroy
Instructed remotely

Not in my name
The abject fear of the distant thunder
The shitting fear of the deafening roar
Shattered homes
Splattered bodies
Splintered lives
Broken homes
Scattered families
Refugees in flight

For what
The death and stench
Of the trenches
The screams of women and children
At Oradour
The horror of the camps
The gulags and killing fields
Have we not learned?

As the desert dust
Settles each night
And each day's death tolls
Are estimated
Five thousand miles away
By the Pentagon
Minor collateral damage
They will say

I cannot avoid the shame
If not the blame

There is no God to forgive
This hubris

This war is not in my name

Judith Elton

written March 2003

Tennysonian Reflections at Barnes Bridge

The river flows before my door,
Sad with sea-gulls, mute with mud
Past Hammersmith and Castelnau,
And strung with barges at the flood.
Pink rowing girls by eight and four
Gently stroke the tide of blood.

A railway runs from side to side
And trains clank over on the hour.
The rowers strain and stretch and slide,
Hair like chrysanthemums, the flower
Of girlhood not yet opened wide,
Each happy in her virgin power.

The dying sun, the dying day
With sunlight charms suburban reaches,
The hackneyed river flows away,
And Time runs too, experience teaches,
Nor for the boring bard will stay
Or rowing girls as fresh as peaches.

Gavin Ewart 1916 -

Stanton Drew

First you dismantle the landscape.
Take away everything you first
Thought of. Trees must go,
Roads of course, the church,
Houses, hedges, livestock, a wire
Fence. The river can stay,
But loses its stubby fringe
Of willows. What do you
See now? Grass, the circling
Mendip rim, with its notches
Fresh like carving. A sky
Like ours, but empty along
Its lower levels. And earth
Stripped of its future, tilted
Into meaning by these stones,
Pitted and unemphatic. Re-create them.
They are the most permanent
Presences here, but cattle, weather,
Archaeologists have rubbed against them.
Still in season they will
Hold the winter sun poised
Over Maes Knoll's white cheek,
Chain the moon's footsteps to
The pattern of their dance.
Stand inside the circle. Put
Your hand on stone. Listen
To the past's long pulse.

U A Fanthorpe 1929 -

Morning has broken

Morning has broken
Like the first morning,
Blackbird has spoken
Like the first bird.
Praise for the singing,
Praise for the morning,
Praise for them springing
Fresh from the Word.

Sweet the rain's new fall
Sunlit from heaven,
Like the first dewfall
On the first grass.
Praise for the sweetness
Of the wet garden,
Sprung in completeness
Where his feet pass.

Mine is the sunlight,
Mine is the morning
Born of the one light
Eden saw play.
Praise with elation,
Praise every morning,
God's re-creation
Of the new day.

Eleanor Farjeon 1881 – 1965

Tree at my Window

Tree at my window, window tree,
My sash is lowered when night comes on;
But let there never be curtain drawn
Between you and me.

Vague dream-head lifted out of the ground,
And thing next most diffuse to cloud,
Not all your light tongues talking aloud
Could be profound.

But tree, I have seen you taken and tossed,
And if you have seen me when I slept,
You have seen me when I was taken and swept
And all but lost.

That day she put our heads together,
Fate had her imagination about her,
Your head so much concerned with outer,
Mine with inner, weather.

Robert Frost 1875 – 1963

Breakfast

We ate our breakfast lying on our backs
Because the shells were screeching overhead.
I bet a rasher to a loaf of bread
That Hull United would beat Halifax
When Jimmy Stainthorpe played full-back instead
Of Billy Bradford. Ginger raised his head
And cursed, and took the bet, and dropped back dead.
We ate our breakfast lying on our backs
Because the shells were screeching overhead.

Wilfrid Gibson 1878 – 1962

Eruptions and Other Dislocations

Herculaneum, a bit later

They've made a good job of the restoration.
I'd half expected Hiroshima:
But they've planted umbrella pines,
Palm-trees, tamarisks,
Eschewed rhododendron, bourgainvillea –
It's pleasant here away from the town
And a dozen other places in this bawling
Half-constructed coastal conurbation:
So what's missing,
What's the absence at the heart
Of the carefully supported half-balconies,
The hints of mural frescoes seen
Through welcome shadowed doors,
Trompe d'oeil drapery,
Vistas in strong dark red on lucent grey
And phosphorescent black?

We the intelligent despise tourists,
Caricature professional site-tickers,
Deplore school parties of sixty
Who don't seem to appreciate
The excerpts manicured with care
For those who have prepaid by credit card;
But if it weren't for expensive curiosity,
Would anyone have bothered to peel
Cubic miles of mud, ash, lava, humus
And assorted rubble off this seashore
Suburban field, to lay bare a few dozen

Bones of a murdered municipal corpse?
Let's at least share a minute's silence:
Tragedy one was the sudden decease
Of a living noisy classical cosmopolis;
The second is the permanent enshrining
(For those who are here for only half a day)
Of what would sooner or later
Have fallen down, been replaced
With something a bit more modern.
(Did they have time to repaint the living-room
For its appearance twenty centuries later?)

And all at once I knew what wasn't there,
What nobody had excavated, nor ever could –
So I climbed up on to a sort of wall,
Seized a megaphone from a guide:

'Everyone here please join in an experiment!
All expectant mothers and children under ten
May stay as they are; the rest of us,
Including tour leaders, academics,
Anyone with a guide book or worksheet,
May choose an age between ten and sixty,
And on the count of three we will all
Stop talking about this ruined town,
And chat instead about everyday things,
Food prices, the weather, goddesses,
Yesterday's production at the theatre,
Who to vote for at the elections,
And whether next week's game
Will be another win for the home side.

In fact, you can talk about anything
You have on your mind and heart and soul –
As long as it's what you would have
Said (or thought) if you'd been living here.'

Well, of course, I didn't have the nerve;
But supposing I did, even so,
Wouldn't the jeans and tee-shirts,
Spectacles and printed books,
Cameras, binoculars, mobile phones
And car keys jangling in pockets
Betray the unbridgeable abyss
Between that older world and ours?
So leave them where they are, and leave us too,
To gawp and comment, use barbaric tongues,
Then disappear to clamber into charabancs
And let the lizards goggling round the rocks
Make completely sure, as they failed to do
This morning, there are no local boys
Waiting to pelt them with stones, something
Small boys have done to lizards
For at least three thousand years,
In between eruptions
And other dislocations.

Mark Greenstock   1939 -

Afterwards

When the Present has latched its postern behind my
tremulous stay,
And the May month flaps its glad green leaves like wings,
Delicate-filmed as new-spun silk, will the neighbours say,
'He was a man who used to notice such things'?

If it be in the dusk when, like an eyelid's soundless blink,
The dewfall-hawk comes crossing the shades to alight
Upon the wind-warped upland thorn, a gazer may think,
'To him this must have been a familiar sight.'

If I pass during some nocturnal blackness,
mothy and warm,
When the hedgehog travels furtively over the lawn,
One may say, 'He strove that such innocent creatures
should come to no harm,
But he could do little for them; and now he is gone.'

If, when hearing that I have been stilled at last,
they stand at the door,
Watching the full-starred heavens that winter sees,
Will this thought rise on those who will meet
my face no more,
'He was one who had an eye for such mysteries'?

And will any say when my bell of quittance is heard in the gloom,
And a crossing breeze cuts a pause in its outrollings,
Till they raise again, as they were a new bell's boom,
'He hears it not now, but used to notice such things?'

Thomas Hardy 1840 – 1928

The Darkling Thrush

I leant upon a coppice gate
    When Frost was spectre-grey,
And Winter's dregs made desolate
    The weakening eye of day.
The tangled bine-stems scored the sky
    Like strings of broken lyres,
And all mankind that haunted nigh
    Had sought their household fires.

The land's sharp features seemed to be
    The Century's corpse out leant,
His crypt the cloudy canopy,
    The wind his death-lament.
The ancient pulse of germ and birth
    Was shrunken hard and dry,
And every spirit upon earth
    Seemed fervourless as I.

At once a voice arose among
	The bleak twigs overhead
In a full-hearted evensong
	Of joy illimited;
And age'd thrush, frail, gaunt, and small,
	In blast-beruffled plume,
Had chosen thus to fling his soul
	Upon the growing gloom.

So little cause for carolings
	Of such ecstatic sound
Was written on terrestrial things
	Afar or nigh around,
That I could think there trembled through
	His happy good-night air
Some blessed Hope, whereof he knew
	And I was unaware.

Thomas Hardy

Cat

Unfussy lodger, she knows what she wants and gets it:
Food, cushions, fires, the run of the garden.
I, her night porter in the small hours
Don't bother to grumble, grimly let her in.
To that coldness she purrs assent,
Eats her fill and outwits me,
Plays hide and seek in the dark house.

Only at times, by chance meeting the gaze
Of her amber eyes that can rest on me
As on a beech-bole, on bracken or meadow grass
I'm moved to celebrate the years between us,
The farness and the nearness:
My fingers graze her head.
To that fondness she purrs assent.

Michael Hamburger 1924 -

Gathering Hazelnuts

Gathering hazelnuts along the road
The last ones poised to fall
I picked and pocketed them.
An explosion of pigeons out of the trees
Turmoiled tremble of upturned leaves
The moon like a tarnished silver dish
Just rising. The sky was watercoloured crudely
Clouds like smoke tinged underneath
With dying flames; sheep like bleached boulders
The fields I knew their names – each one
Like friends with whom I shared
Memories of springtime, harvest, rolling love.
Venus inhabited her own space among
Shredded clouds torn from a herring-bone sky
Spirits hung above the Saxon tower, bats
Skimmed across graves for moths and I alone
Saw nicotine stains around the moon.

Jane Henriques 1944 -

Delight in Disorder

A sweet disorder in the dresse
Kindles in cloathes a wantonnesse:
A Lawne about the shoulders thrown
Into a fine distraction:
An erring Lace, which here and there
Enthralls the Crimson Stomacher:
A Cuffe neglectfull, and thereby
Ribbands to flow confusedly:
A winning wave (deserving Note)
In the tempestuous petticote:
A carelesse shooe-string, in whose tye
I see a wilde civility:
Doe more bewitch me, than when Art
Is too precise in every part.

Robert Herrick 1591 – 1674

To Daffodils

Fair Daffodils, we weep to see
You haste away so soon:
As yet the early-rising Sun
Has not attain'd his noon.

Stay, Stay,
Until the hasting day
Has run
But to the even-song;
And, having pray'd together, we
Will go with you along.

We have short time to stay, as you,
We have as short a Spring;
As quick a growth to meet decay
As you, or any thing.
We die,
As your hours do, and dry
Away
Like to the Summer's rain;
Or as the pearls of morning's dew
Ne'er to be found again.

Robert Herrick

Counsel to Girls

Gather ye rose-buds while ye may,
Old Time is still a-flying:
And this same flower that smiles to-day,
To-morrow will be dying.

The glorious Lamp of Heaven, the Sun,
The higher he's a-getting
The sooner will his race be run,
And nearer he's to setting.

That age is best which is the first,
When youth and blood are warmer:
But being spent, the worse, and worst
Times, will succeed the former.

Then be not coy, but use your time;
And while ye may, go marry:
For having lost but once your prime,
You may for ever tarry.

Robert Herrick

The Flowers

After lunch my daughter picked
handfuls of the wild flowers
she knew her grandfather liked best
and piled them in the basket of her bicycle,
beside an empty jam-jar and a trowel;
then, swaying like a candle-bearer,
she rode off to the church
and, like a little dog, I followed her.

She cleared the grave of nettles
and wild parsley, and dug a shallow hole
to put the jam-jar in. She arranged
the flowers to look their best
and scraped the moss from the stone,
so you could see whose grave
she had been caring for.
It didn't take long – no longer
than making his bed in the morning
when he had got too old to help her.

Not knowing how to leave him,
how to say goodbye, I hesitated
by the rounded grave. Come on,
my daughter said, it's finished now.
And so we got our bicycles and rode home
down the lane, moving apart
and coming together again,
in and out of the ruts.

Selima Hill 1945 -

I Remember, I Remember

I remember, I remember,
The house where I was born,
The little window where the sun
Came peeping in at morn;
He never came a wink too soon,
Nor brought too long a day,
But now, I often wish the night
Had borne my breath away.

I remember, I remember,
The roses, red and white;
The violets, and the lily-cups,
Those flowers made of light!
The lilacs where the robin built,
And where my brother set
The laburnum on his birthday -
The tree is living yet!

I remember, I remember,
Where I used to swing;
And thought the air must rush as fresh
To swallows on the wing:
My spirit flew in feathers then,
That is so heavy now,
And summer pools could hardly cool
The fever on my brow!

I remember, I remember,
The fir trees dark and high;
I used to think their slender tops
Were close against the sky:
It was a childish ignorance,
But now 'tis little joy
To know I'm farther off from Heav'n
Than when I was a boy.

Thomas Hood 1799 – 1845

Pied Beauty

Glory be to God for dappled things -
  For skies of couple-colour as a brinded cow;
    For rose-moles all in stipple upon trout that swim;
Fresh-firecoal chestnut-falls; finches' wings;
  Landscape plotted and pieced - fold, fallow, and
plough;
    And áll trádes, their gear and tackle and trim.

All things counter, original, spare, strange;
  Whatever is fickle, freckled (who knows how?)
    With swift, slow; sweet, sour; adazzle, dim;
He fathers-forth whose beauty is past change:
    Praise him.

Gerald Manley Hopkins 1844 - 1889

The Windhover

To Christ our Lord

I caught this morning morning's minion, kingdom of
daylight's dauphin, dapple-dawn-drawn Falcon,
  in his riding
Of the rolling level underneath him steady air, and striding
High there, how he rung upon the rein of a wimpling wing
In his ecstasy! then off, off forth on swing,
As a skate's heel sweeps smooth on a bow-bend:
the hurl and gliding
Rebuffed the big wind. My heart in hiding
Stirred for a bird, - the achieve of, the mastery of the thing!

Brute beauty and valour and act, oh, air, pride, plume, here
Buckle! And the fire that breaks from thee then, a billion
Times told lovelier, more dangerous, O my chevalier!

No wonder of it: shéer plód makes plough down sillion
Shine, and blue-bleak embers, ah my dear,
Fall, gall themselves, and gash gold-vermilion.

Gerald Manley Hopkins

Inversnaid

This darksome burn, horseback brown,
His rollrock highroad roaring down,
In coop and in comb the fleece of his foam
Flutes and low to the lake falls home.

A windpuff-bonnet of fawn-froth
Turns and twindles over the broth
Of a pool so pitchblack, fell-frowning,
It rounds and rounds Despair to drowning.

Degged with dew, dappled with dew,
Are the groins of the braes that the brook treads
through,
Wiry heathpacks, flitches of fern,
And the beadbonny ash that sits over the burn.

What would the world be, once bereft
Of wet and wildness? Let them be left,
O let them be left, wildness and wet;
Long live the weeds and the wilderness yet.

Gerald Manley Hopkins

Loveliest of Trees, The Cherry Now

Loveliest of trees, the cherry now
Is hung with bloom along the bough,
And stands about the woodland ride
Wearing white for Eastertide.
Now, of my threescore years and ten,
Twenty will not come again,
And take from seventy springs a score,
It only leaves me fifty more.

And since to look at things in bloom
Fifty springs are little room,
About the woodlands I will go
To see the cherry hung with snow.

A E Housman 1859 – 1936

To Celia

Drinke to me, only, with thine eyes,
And I will pledge with mine;
Or leave a kisse but in the cup,
And Ile not looke for wine.
The thirst, that from the soule doth rise,
Doth aske a drinke divine:
But might I of Jove's Nectar sup,
I would not change for thine.
I sent thee, late, a rosie wreath,
Not so much honoring thee,
As giving it a hope, that there
It could not withered bee.
But thou thereon did'st onely breath,
And sent'st it back to mee:
Since when it growes, and smells, I sweare,
Not of it selfe, but thee.

Ben Jonson 1572 - 1637

Warning

When I am an old woman I shall wear purple
With a red hat which doesn't go, and doesn't suit me,
And I shall spend my pension on brandy and summer gloves
And satin sandals, and say we've no money for butter.
I shall sit down on the pavement when I'm tired
And gobble up samples in shops and press alarm bells
And run my stick along the public railings
And make up for the sobriety of my youth.
I shall go out in my slippers in the rain
And pick the flowers in other people's gardens
And learn to spit.

You can wear terrible shirts and grow more fat
And eat three pounds of sausages at a go
Or only bread and pickle for a week
And hoard pens and pencils and beermats
and things in boxes.
But now we must have clothes that keep us dry
And pay our rent and not swear in the street
And set a good example for the children.
We will have friends to dinner and read the papers.
But maybe I ought to practise a little now?
So people who know me are not too shocked and surprised
When suddenly I am old and start to wear purple.

Jenny Joseph 1932 -

Ithaca

When you set out on your journey to Ithaca,
pray that the road is long,
full of adventure, full of knowledge.
The Lestrygonians and the Cyclops,
the angry Poseidon — do not fear them:
You will never find such as these on your path,
if your thoughts remain lofty, if a fine
emotion touches your spirit and your body.
The Lestrygonians and the Cyclops,
the fierce Poseidon you will never encounter,
if you do not carry them within your soul,
if your soul does not set them up before you.

Pray that the road is long.
That the summer mornings are many, when,
with such pleasure, with such joy
you will enter ports seen for the first time;
stop at Phoenician markets,
and purchase fine merchandise,
mother-of-pearl and coral, amber and ebony,
and sensual perfumes of all kinds,
as many sensual perfumes as you can;
visit many Egyptian cities,
to learn and learn from scholars.

Always keep Ithaca in your mind.
To arrive there is your ultimate goal.
But do not hurry the voyage at all.
It is better to let it last for many years;
and to anchor at the island when you are old,
rich with all you have gained on the way,
not expecting that Ithaca will offer you riches.

Ithaca has given you the beautiful voyage.
Without her you would have never set out on the road.
She has nothing more to give you.

And if you find her poor, Ithaca has not deceived you.
Wise as you have become, with so much experience,
you must already have understood what Ithacas mean.

C P Kavafis 1863 – 1933

Wet Evening in April

The birds sang in the wet trees
And as I listened to them it was a hundred years from now
And I was dead and someone else was listening to them.
But I was glad I had recorded for him
The melancholy.

Patrick Kavanagh 1905 – 1967

Thoughts on a French Graveyard

This at last is petrification;
Death and final mortification
Of living substance, condemned to lie
Beneath the soil.
How the stone slabs
Glare bleakly above the ground
Like sentinels grimly keeping watch
On their unresisting charges.

Between these silent graves,   .
An occasional cluster of flowers;
Gleaming and bright, nor yet subdued
By those spectral stone watchmen.
The grass verges are trimly kept,
Paths winding meticulously through the graves
Of those long since dead and buried,
Ashes to ashes, dust to dust.

They came here in their thousands
Through the glory of the war.
Heroes mortally wounded then forgotten
When the trenches had long been filled in.
Yet homage is paid to those who gave
Their lives, ideals still remembered –
By those who living now are waiting too –
For the final undeniable surrender.

Patricia Kilshaw   1945 -

from An Exequy on his Wife

Sleep on (my Love!) in thy cold bed
Never to be disquieted.
My last Good-night! Thou wilt not wake
Till I Thy Fate shall overtake:
Till age, or grief, or sickness must
Marry my Body to that Dust
It so much loves; and fill the roome
My heart keepes empty in Thy Tomb.
Stay for mee there: I will not faile
To meet Thee in that hollow Vale.
And think not much of my delay;
I am already on the way,
And follow Thee with all the speed
Desire can make, or Sorrowes breed.
Each Minute is a short Degree
And e'ry Howre a stepp towards Thee.
At Night when I betake to rest,
Next Morne I rise neerer my West
Of Life, almost by eight Howres sayle,
Then when Sleep breath'd his drowsy gale.
Thus from the Sunne my Bottome steares,
And my Daye's Compasse downward beares.
Nor labour I to stemme the Tide,
Through which to Thee I swiftly glide.
'Tis true; with shame and grief I yield
Thou, like the Vann, first took'st the Field,
And gotten hast the Victory
In thus adventuring to Dy
Before Mee; whose more yeeres might crave
A just precedence in the Grave.

But hark! My Pulse, like a soft Drum
Beates my Approach, Tells Thee I come;
And, slowe howe're my Marches bee,
I shall at last sitt downe by Thee.
The thought of this bids mee goe on,
And wait my dissolution
With Hope and Comfort. Deare! (forgive
The Crime) I am content to live
Divided, with but half a Heart,
Till wee shall Meet and Never part.

Henry King 1592 – 1669

Churchgoing

What superstitions have their thrones
Within these shaped and pitted stones
Beside which on each holy day
With others I have knelt to pray?

For centuries the tower bell
Called people here by whom the hell
Of priest and prayer book was more feared
Than lives of hardship which they shared.

Now I who come here cannot find
Belief in hell beyond the mind
And body. If that does not start
What value has its counterpart?

But here with my selective creed
I find, unhoping, peace I need,
Sing unconvinced of angel hosts
And kneel with my forefathers' ghosts.

Walter Kemsley   1915 -

Marshes

Each marsh that I have known displays
The looks of others. Each recedes
On levels crossed by waterways
Whose whispering wind-ruffled reeds
Accompany the skylark's song
And curlew's intermittent call
Which makes space sad. Perhaps along
Some inland edge daylight's last fall
Is snared by woods already dark
Before night steals the background hills
And, nearer, casts its masking cloak
On sheep and settled geese, and fills
The creeks where tidal waters creep.
Yet in my thoughts no rays of dawn
Caress the reed or stir the sheep
Except hard by where I was born
And where I first breathed salt marsh air
When as a child I went to play
By ragged ewes and peewits there-
In years and miles now far away.

Walter Kemsley

Annus Mirabilis

Sexual intercourse began
In nineteen sixty-three
(Which was rather late for me) -
Between the end of the Chatterley ban
And the Beatles' first LP.

Up till then there'd only been
A sort of bargaining,
A wrangle for a ring,
A shame that started at sixteen
And spread to everything.

Then all at once the quarrel sank:
Everyone felt the same,
And every life became
A brilliant breaking of the bank,
A quite unlosable game.

So life was never better than
In nineteen sixty-three
(Though just too late for me) -
Between the end of the Chatterley ban
And the Beatles' first LP.

Philip Larkin 1922 – 1985

This be the Verse

They fuck you up, your mum and dad.
They may not mean to, but they do.
They fill you with the faults they had
And add some extra, just for you.

But they were fucked up in their turn
By fools in old-style hats and coats,
Who half the time were soppy-stern
And half at one another's throats.

Man hands on misery to man.
It deepens like a coastal shelf.
Get out as early as you can,
And don't have any kids yourself.

Philip Larkin

The Owl and the Pussy-Cat

The Owl and the Pussy-Cat went to sea
  In a beautiful pea-green boat,
They took some honey, and plenty of money,
  Wrapped up in a five-pound note.
The Owl looked up to the stars above,
  And sang to a small guitar.
'O lovely Pussy! O Pussy, my love,
  What a beautiful Pussy you are,
    You are,
    You are!
  What a beautiful Pussy you are!'

Pussy said to the Owl, 'You elegant fowl!
  How charmingly sweet you sing!
O let us be married! too long we have tarried:
  But what shall we do for a ring?'
They sailed away for a year and a day,
  To the land where the Bong-tree grows,
And there in a wood a Piggy-wig stood,
  With a ring at the end of his nose,
    His nose,
    His nose,
  With a ring at the end of his nose.

'Dear Pig, are you willing to sell for one shilling
   Your ring?' Said the Piggy, 'I will.'
So they took it away, and were married next day
   By the Turkey who lives on the hill.

They dinèd on mince, and slices of quince,
   Which they ate with a runcible spoon;
And hand in hand, on the edge of the sand,
   They danced by the light of the moon,
      The moon,
      The moon,
   They danced by the light of the moon,

Edward Lear 1812 – 1888

Snow

The room was suddenly rich and the great bay-
window was
Spawning snow and pink roses against it
Soundlessly collateral and incompatible:
World is suddener than we fancy it.

World is crazier and more of it than we think,
Incorrigibly plural. I peel and portion
A tangerine and spit the pips and feel
The drunkenness of things being various.

And the fire flames with a bubbling sound for world
Is more spiteful and gay than one supposes -
On the tongue on the eyes on the ears in the palms of
one's hands -
There is more than glass between the snow and the
huge roses.

Louis MacNiece 1907 - 1963

From Bagpipe Music

It's no go my honey love, it's no go my poppet;
Work your hands from day to day, the winds will
blow the profit.
The glass is falling hour by hour, the glass will fall for
ever,
But if you break the bloody glass you won't hold up
the weather.

Louis MacNiece

High Flight (An Airman's Ecstasy)

Oh, I have slipped the surly bonds of earth
And danced the skies on laughter-silvered wings;
Sunward I've climbed and joined the tumbling mirth
Of sun-split clouds - and done a hundred things
You have not dreamed of; wheeled and soared and
swung
High in the sun-lit silence. Hovering there
I've chased the shouting wind along, and flung
My eager craft through footless halls of air;
Up, up the long, delirious, burning blue
I've topped the wind-swept heights with easy grace,
Where never lark nor even eagle flew;
And while, with silent lifting mind I've trod
The high untrespassed sanctity of space,
Put out my hand, and touched the face of God.

John Gillespie Magee 1921 – 1941

The Life That I Have

The life that I have
Is all that I have
And the life that I have
Is yours

The love that I have
Of the life that I have
Is yours and yours and yours

A sleep I shall have
A rest I shall have
Yet death will be but a pause

For the peace of my years
In the long green grass
Will be yours and yours and yours

Leo Marks 1920 -

The Passionate Shepherd to his Love

Come live with me and be my Love,
And we will all the pleasures prove
That hills and valleys, dale and field,
And all the craggy mountains yield.

There will we sit upon the rocks
And see the shepherds feed their flocks,
By shallow rivers, to whose falls
Melodious birds sing madrigals.

There will I make thee beds of roses
And a thousand fragrant posies,
A cap of flowers, and a kirtle
Embroider'd all with leaves of myrtle.

A gown made of the finest wool,
Which from our pretty lambs we pull,
Fair linéd slippers for the cold,
With buckles of the purest gold.

A belt of straw and ivy buds
With coral clasps and amber studs:
And if these pleasures may thee move,
Come live with me and be my Love.

Thy silver dishes for thy meat
As precious as the gods do eat,
Shall on an ivory table be
Prepared each day for thee and me.

The shepherd swains shall dance and sing
For thy delight each May-morning:
If these delights thy mind may move,
Then live with me and be my love.

Christopher Marlowe 1564 – 1593

To His Coy Mistress

Had we but World enough, and Time,
This coyness Lady were no crime.
We would sit down, and think which way
To walk, and pass our long Loves Day.
Thou by the Indian Ganges side
Should'st Rubies find: I by the Tide
Of Humber would complain. I would
Love you ten years before the Flood:
And you should if you please refuse
Till the Conversion of the Jews.
My vegetable Love should grow
Vaster than Empires, and more slow.
An hundred years should go to praise
Thine Eyes, and on thy Forehead Gaze.
Two hundred to adore each Breast:
But thirty thousand to the rest.
An Age at least to every part,
And the last Age should show your Heart.
For Lady you deserve this State;
Nor would I love at lower rate.
But at my back I alwaies hear
Times wingéd Charriot hurrying near:
And yonder all before us lye
Desarts of vast Eternity.
Thy Beauty shall no more be found,
Nor, in thy marble Vault, shall sound
My echoing Song: then Worms shall try
That long preserv'd Virginity:
And your quaint Honour turn to dust;
And into ashes all my Lust.

The Grave's a fine and private place,
But none I think do there embrace.
Now therefore, while the youthful hew
Sits on thy skin like morning dew,
And while thy willing Soul transpires
At every pore with instant Fires,
Now let us sport us while we may;
And now, like am'rous birds of prey,
Rather at once our Time devour,
Than languish in his slow-chapt pow'r.
Let us roll all our Strength, and all
Our sweetness, up into one Ball:
And tear our Pleasures with rough strife,
Thorough the Iron gates of Life.
Thus, though we cannot make our Sun
Stand still, yet we will make him run.

Andrew Marvell 1628 – 1678

Sea-Fever

I must go down to the seas again,
to the lonely sea and the sky,
And all I ask is a tall ship and a star to steer her by,
And the wheel's kick and the wind's song and the
white sail's shaking,
And a grey mist on the sea's face and a grey dawn
breaking.

I must go down to the seas again,
for the call of the running tide
Is a wild call and a clear call that may not be denied;
And all I ask is a windy day with the white clouds
flying,
And the flung spray and the blown spume, and the
sea-gulls crying.

I must go down to the seas again,
to the vagrant gypsy life,
To the gull's way and the whale's way where the
wind's like a whetted knife;
And all I ask is a merry yarn from a
laughing fellow-rover,
And quiet sleep and a sweet dream when the long
trick's over.

John Masefield 1878 – 1967

Up on the Downs

Up on the downs the red-eyed kestrels hover,
Eyeing the grass.
The field-mouse flits like a shadow into cover
As their shadows pass.
Men are burning the gorse on the down's shoulder;
A drift of smoke
Glitters with fire and hangs, and the skies smoulder,
And the lungs choke.

Once the tribe did thus on the downs, on these downs burning
Men in the frame,
Crying to the gods of the downs till their brains were turning
And the gods came.

And to-day on the downs, in the wind, the hawks, the grasses,
In blood and air,
Something passes me and cries as it passes,
On the chalk downland bare.

John Masefield

In Flanders Fields

In Flanders fields the poppies blow
Between the crosses, row on row
That mark our place; and in the sky
The larks, still bravely singing, fly
Scarce heard amid the guns below.

We are the Dead. Short days ago
We lived, felt dawn, saw sunset glow,
Loved and were loved, and now we lie
In Flanders fields.

Take up our quarrel with the foe:
To you from failing hands we throw
The torch; be yours to hold it high.
If ye break faith with us who die
We shall not sleep, though poppies grow
In Flanders Fields.

John McCrea 1872 – 1918

Survivor

Everyday
I think about dying.
About disease, starvation,
violence, terrorism, war,
the end of the world.

It helps
keep my mind off things.

Roger McGough   1937 -

115

A Way to Meet

Little jewel
where something beats alive
in the warm sky
and rises through my heel
on the dog-walked grass

through steep posted pitches
every house links foot with
everywhere
and everywhere under the round and
rising moon is
home

Built, maybe, by some
warm slow folk
whose every name, whether
friend or no
was neighbour
and humble and high
under the damp banks planted
poppies and roses
brick and stone and weavers cots
and rows of high wainscotted rooms
behind peonied facades
cheek by jowl just anyhow
so long as there was always
a way through
a way to meet
and almost never a path
was blind

Could we now with our
drug-eyed young
and telly-tongued labourless
our barterers and dreamers
wearing the patched streets like
ball gowns
striking ideals like green sparks
out of the valley air

with our crazy devoted craft-folk
lackaday poets
and our latter-day wise women
our scratched and wounded healers
skint and hopeful all

could we
defy the brown and brackish tide
of slump and disempowering
and make of this place a pattern
for a different generation
putting the soil back central
letting warmth flood up from
garden and field
beat again under the steep street
so everywhere is home again
and there is always a way
to meet?

Jehanne Mehta 1941 -

117

Toni

We carved our hearts
  on a tree in Graz
  and the hands of the clock stood still.
Down a timeless lane
  I can feel again
  that distant winter chill.
By the Wörther See
  when you came to me
  the wine of life was flowing,
But night and day
  time runs away
  and we know not where it's going.
As must we must
  time turns to dust
Like the long lost day together,
  on our wings of love,
  flew a dying dove
To leave us wondering whether
  that Capri day
  at our feet there lay
The time-drenched Faraglioni.
But the road we ascended
  had finally ended.
  Addio amore, Toni.

Spike Milligan 1918 – 2002

Song. On May Morning

Now the bright morning star, day's harbinger
Comes dancing from the east, and leads with her
The flow'ry May, who from her green lap throws
The yellow cowslip and the pale primrose.
  Hail, bounteous May, that dost inspire
  Mirth, and youth, and warm desire:
  Woods and groves are of thy dressing,
  Hill and dale doth boast thy blessing.
Thus we salute thee with our early song,
And welcome thee, and wish thee long.

John Milton 1608 – 1674

usbands

narriage brimming,
ie loving cup,
're wrong, admit it;
're right, shut up.

02 – 1971

Remember

Remember me when I am gone away,
Gone far away into the silent land;
When you can no more hold me by the hand,
Nor I half turn to go yet turning stay.
Remember me when no more day by day
You tell me of our future that you planned:

Only remember me; you understand
It will be late to counsel then or pray.
Yet if you should forget me for a while
And afterwards remember, do not grieve:
For if the darkness and corruption leave
A vestige of the thoughts that once I had,
Better by far you should forget and smile
Than that you should remember and be sad.

Christina G Rossetti 1830 –1894

In The Bleak Mid Winter

In the bleak mid-winter
Frosty wind made moan,
Earth stood hard as iron,
Water like a stone;
Snow had fallen, snow on snow,
Snow on snow,
In the bleak mid-winter,
Long ago.

Our God, heaven cannot hold him
Nor earth sustain;
Heaven and earth shall flee away
When he comes to reign:
In the bleak mid-winter
A stable-place sufficed
The Lord God Almighty
Jesus Christ.

Enough for him, whom Cherubim
Worship night and day,
A breastful of milk,
And a mangerful of hay;
Enough for him, whom Angels
Fall down before,
The ox and ass and camel
Which adore.

Angels and Archangels
May have gathered there,
Cherubim and Seraphim
Thronged the air –
But only his mother
In her maiden bliss
Worshipped the Belovèd
With a kiss.

What can I give him
Poor as I am?
If I were a shepherd
I would bring a lamb;
If I were a wise man
I would do my part;
Yet what I can I give him –
Give my heart.

Christina G Rossetti

Song

When I am dead, my dearest,
Sing no sad songs for me;
Plant thou no roses at my head,
Nor shady cypress tree:
Be the green grass above me
With showers and dewdrops wet;
And if thou wilt, remember,
And if thou wilt, forget.

I shall not see the shadows,
I shall not feel the rain;
I shall not hear the nightingale
Sing on, as if in pain;
And dreaming through the twilight
That doth not rise nor set,
Haply I may remember
And haply may forget.

Christina G Rossetti

The Author's Epitaph, Made by Himselfe

Even such is Time, which takes in trust
Our Youth, our Joys, and all we have,
And payes us but with age and dust,
Who in the darke and silent grave,
When we have wandred all our wayes,
Shuts up the story of our dayes:
And from which Earth, and Grave, and Dust,
The Lord shall raise me up I trust.

Sir Walter Ralegh 1542 – 1618

Everyone Sang

Everyone suddenly burst out singing;
And I was filled with such delight
As prisoned birds must find in freedom
Winging wildly across the white
Orchards and dark-green fields; on – on - and out
  of sight.

Everyone's voice was suddenly lifted
And beauty came like the setting sun.
My heart was shaken with tears; and horror
Drifted away... O but Everyone
Was a bird; and the song was wordless; the singing
  will never be done.

Siegfried Sassoon 1886 – 1967

126

Seven Ages

All the world's a stage,
And all the men and women merely players:
They have their exits and their entrances;
And one man in his time plays many parts,
His acts being seven ages. At first the infant,
Mewling and puking in the nurse's arms.
Then the whining school-boy, with his satchel
And shining morning face, creeping like snail
Unwillingly to school. And then the lover,
Sighing like furnace, with a woeful ballad
Made to his mistress' eyebrow. Then a soldier,
Full of strange oaths, and bearded like the pard,
Jealous in honour, sudden and quick in quarrel,
Seeking the bubble reputation
Even in the cannon's mouth. And then the justice,
In fair round belly with good capon lined,
With eyes severe and beard of formal cut,
Full of wise saws and modern instances;
And so he plays his part. The sixth age shifts
Into the lean and slipper'd pantaloon,
With spectacles on nose and pouch on side,
His youthful hose, well saved, a world too wide
For his shrunk shank; and his big manly voice,
Turning again toward childish treble, pipes
And whistles in his sound. Last scene of all,
That ends this strange eventful history,
Is second childishness, and mere oblivion,
Sans teeth, sans eyes, sans taste, sans everything.

William Shakespeare 1564 –1616

Let me not to the marriage of true mindes
Admit impediments, love is not love
Which alters when it alteration findes,
Or bends with the remover to remove.
O no, it is an ever fixed marke
That lookes on tempests and is never shaken;
It is the star to every wandring barke,
Whose worths unknowne, although his higth be taken.
Lov's not Times foole, though rosie lips and cheeks
Within his bending sickles compasse come,
Love alters not with his breefe houres and weekes,
But beares it out even to the edge of doome:
  If this be error and upon me proved,
  I never writ, nor no man ever loved.

William Shakespeare

Like as the waves make towards the pebbled shore,
So do our minuites hasten to their end,
Each changing place with that which goes before,
In sequent toile all forwards do contend.
Nativity once in the maine of light
Crawles to maturity, wherewith being crown'd,
Crooked eclipses gainst his glory fight,
And time that gave, doth now his gift confound.
Time doth transfixe the florish set on youth,
And delves the paralels in beauties brow,
Feedes on the rarities of natures truth,
And nothing stands but for his sieth to mow.
   And yet to times in hope, my verse shall stand
   Praising thy worth, dispight his cruell hand.

William Shakespeare

To His Love

Shall I compare thee to a summer's day?
Thou art more lovely and more temperate:
Rough windes do shake the darling buds of Maie,
And Sommer's lease hath all too short a date.
Sometime too hot the eye of heaven shines
And often is his gold complexion dimm'd:
And every faire from faire some-time declines,
By chance, or nature's changing course, untrimm'd.
But thy eternal summer shall not fade
Nor lose possession of that fair thou ow'st;
Nor shall death brag thou wandr'st in his shade,
When in eternal lines to time thou grow'st;
  So long as men can breathe, or eyes can see,
  So long lives this, and this gives life to thee.

William Shakespeare

That time of yeeare thou maist in me behold,
When yellow leaves, or none, or few doe hange
Upon those boughs which shake against the could,
Bare ruin'd quiers, where late the sweet birds sang.
In me thou seest the twi-light of such day,
As after Sun-set fadeth in the West,
Which by and by blacke night doth take away,
Deaths second selfe that seals up all in rest.
In me thou seest the glowing of such fire,
That on the ashes of his youth doth lye,
As the death-bed, whereon it must expire,
Consum'd with that which it was nurrisht by.
  This thou percev'st, which makes thy love more
strong,
    To love that well, which thou must leave ere long.

William Shakespeare

Art, Art, Amazing Art

Art, art, amazing art,
Marbling like colourful veins stretching out,
Tie-dye, an explosion to make you shout.

Art, art, brilliant art,
Tremendous tattoos and studs like pearls,
Henna – like patterns in rusty swirls.

Art, art, fantastic art,
Marvellous mosaics are ripped stone carpets,
Sculptured pots are admired in markets.

Art, art, beautiful art,
Charcoal in night smudged into dawn,
Collage the sticky jigsaw torn.

Ellie Sterling 1993 -

132

Requiem

Under the wide and starry sky,
Dig the grave and let me lie.
Glad did I live and gladly die,
And I laid me down with a will.

This be the verse you grave for me:
Here he lies where he longed to be;
Home is the sailor, home from sea,
And the hunter home from the hill.

Robert Louis Stevenson 1850 – 1894

Break, Break, Break

Break, break, break
　On thy cold grey stones, O Sea!
And I would that my tongue could utter
　The thoughts that arise in me.

O well for the fisherman's boy,
　That he shouts with his sister at play!
O well for the sailor lad,
　That he sings in his boat on the bay!

And the stately ships go on
　To their haven under the hill;
But O for the touch of a vanish'd hand,
　And the sound of a voice that is still!

Break, break, break
　At the foot of thy crags, O Sea!
But the tender grace of a day that is dead
　Will never come back to me.

Alfred Lord Tennyson 1809 – 1892

Crossing the Bar

Sunset and evening star,
　And one clear call for me.
And may there be no moaning of the bar,
　When I put out to sea,

But such a tide as moving seems asleep,
　Too full for sound and foam,
When that which drew from out the boundless deep
　Turns again home.

Twilight and evening bell,
　And after that the dark:
And may there be no sadness of farewell,
　When I embark;

For tho' from out our bourne of Time and Place
　The flood may bear me far,
I hope to see my Pilot face to face,
　When I have crost the bar.

Alfred Lord Tennyson

Do not go gentle into that good night

Do not go gentle into that good night,
Old age should burn and rave at close of day;
Rage, rage against the dying of the light.

Though wise men at their end know dark is right,
Because their words had forked no lightning they
Do not go gentle into that good night.

Good men, the last wave by, crying how bright
Their frail deeds might have danced in a green bay,
Rage, rage against the dying of the light.

Wild men who caught and sang the sun in flight,
And learn, too late, they grieved it on its way,
Do not go gentle into that good night.

Grave men, near death, who see with blinding sight
Blind eyes could blaze like meteors and be gay,
Rage, rage against the dying of the light.

And you, my father, there on the sad height,
Curse, bless, me now with your fierce tears, I pray.
Do not go gentle into that good night.
Rage, rage against the dying of the light.

Dylan Thomas 1914 – 1953

Fern Hill

Now as I was young and easy under the apple boughs
About the lilting house and happy as the grass was green,
    The night above the dingle starry,
    Time let me hail and climb
    Golden in the heydays of his eyes,
And honoured among wagons I was prince of the apple towns
And once below a time I lordly had the trees and leaves
    Trail with daisies and barley
    Down the rivers of the windfall light.

And as I was green and carefree, famous among the barns
About the happy yard and singing as the farm was home,
    In the sun that is young once only,
    Time let me play and be
    Golden in the mercy of his means,
And green and golden I was huntsman and herdsman, and calves
Sang to my horn, the foxes on the hills barked clear and cold,
    And the sabbath rang slowly
    In the pebbles of the holy streams.

All the sun long it was running, it was lovely, the hay
Fields high as the house, the tunes from the chimneys, it was air
    And playing, lovely and watery
    And fire green as grass.
    And nightly under the simple stars
As I rode to sleep the owls were bearing the farm away,

All the moon long I heard, blessed among stables,
the night-jars
	Flying with the ricks, and the horses
	Flashing into the dark.

And then to awake, and the farm, like a wanderer white
With the dew, come back, the cock on his shoulder:
it was all
	Shining, it was Adam and maiden,
	The sky gathered again
	And the sun grew round that very day,
So it must have been after the birth of the simple light
In the first, spinning place, the spellbound horses walking
warm
	Out of the whinnying green stable
	On to the fields of praise.

And honoured among foxes and pheasants by the gay
house
Under the new made clouds and happy as the heart was
long,
	In the sun born over and over,
	I ran my heedless ways,
	My wishes raced through the house high hay
And nothing I cared, at my sky blue trades, that time
allows
In all his tuneful turning so few and such morning songs
	Before the children green and golden
	Follow him out of grace.

Nothing I cared, in the lamb white days, that time
would take me
Up to the swallow thronged loft by the shadow of my
hand,
    In the moon that is always rising,
    Nor that riding to sleep
    I should hear him fly with the high fields
And wake to the farm forever fled from the childless
land.
Oh as I was young and easy in the mercy of his means,
    Time held me green and dying
    Though I sang in my chains like the sea.

Dylan Thomas

Poem in October

It was my thirtieth year to heaven
Woke to my hearing from harbour and neighbour
wood
And the mussel pooled and the heron
Priested shore
The morning beckon
With water praying and call of seagull and rook
And the knock of sailing boats on the net webbed wall
Myself to set afoot
That second
In the still sleeping town and set forth.

My birthday began with the water–
Birds and the birds of the wing'd trees flying my name
Above the farms and the white horses
And I rose
In the rainy autumn
And walked abroad in a shower of all my days.
High tide and the heron dived when I took the road
Over the border
And the gates
Of the town closed as the town awoke.

A springful of larks in a rolling
Cloud and the roadside bushes brimming with
whistling
Blackbirds and the sun of October
Summery
On the hill's shoulder,
Here were fond climates and sweet singers suddenly

Come in the morning where I wandered and listened
To the rain wringing
Wind blow cold
In the wood faraway under me.

Pale rain over the dwindling harbour
And over the sea wet church the size of a snail
With its horns through mist and the castle
Brown as owls
But all the gardens
Of spring and summer were blooming in the tall tales
Beyond the border and under the lark full of cloud.
There could I marvel
My birthday
Away but the weather turned around.

It turned away from the blithe country
And down the other air and the blue altered sky
Streamed again a wonder of summer
With apples
Pears and red currants
And I saw in the turning so clearly a child's
Forgotten mornings when he walked with his mother
Through the parables
Of sun light
And the legends of the green chapels

And the twice told fields of infancy
That his tears burned my cheeks and his heart moved
in mine.
These were the woods the river and sea
Where a boy
In the listening
Summertime of the dead whispered the truth of his joy
To the trees and the stones and the fish in the tide.
And the mystery
Sang alive
Still in the water and singing birds.

And there could I marvel my birthday
Away but the weather turned around. And the true
Joy of the long dead child sang burning
In the sun.
It was my thirtieth
Year to heaven stood there in the summer noon
Though the town below lay leaved with October
blood.
O may my heart's truth
Still be sung
On this high hill in a year's turning.

Dylan Thomas

Thaw

Over the land freckled with snow half-thawed
The speculating rooks at their nests cawed
And saw from elm-tops, delicate as flower of grass,
What we below could not see, Winter pass.

Edward Thomas 1878 – 1917

Adlestrop

Yes, I remember Adlestrop -
The name, because one afternoon
Of heat the express-train drew up there
Unwontedly. It was late June.

The steam hissed. Someone cleared his throat.
No one left and no one came
On the bare platform. What I saw
Was Adlestrop - only the name

And willows, willow-herb, and grass,
And meadowsweet, and haycocks dry,
Not whit less still and lonely fair
Than the high cloudlets in the sky.

And for that minute a blackbird sang
Close by, and round him, mistier,
Farther and farther, all the birds
Of Oxfordshire and Gloucestershire.

Edward Thomas

Middle Years

I reach middle years
Transforming like a pupa
More slowly than trees
Slower even than a stone
I hope there is time
For wings to unfurl in the sun

Paul Thornycroft 1949 -

Temple Flags

Temple flags flutter
Spirit, breath of God visible
Pilgrims come forever

Paul Thornycroft

Folding Hills

This summer evening
Folding hills melt together
In velvet quiet

Paul Thornycroft

Untitled

Love be the sun that stirs in me
The immanence of sight,
And may my affirmation be
The cool response of flower to light.

Needs it a faith articulate
That life within its being grows?
Is there a doubt that dawn will greet
The dusk-begotten rose?

Love speaks to life in me no less
In confident reply,
Distilling from all subtleness
Its clear simplicity.

Vera Titmuss 1909 – 1993

The Summer Spills her Treasure

The summer spills her treasure
As mist on winter sun,
Pain follows close on pleasure.

Joy suffers time's erasure:
All ends that is begun:
The summer spills her treasure.

For heirs to gilded leisure
Or fate unkindly spun
Pain follows close on pleasure.

The spring smiles like a geisha
The autumn like a nun:
The summer spills her treasure.

In plundered fields the thresher,
In leafless woods and gun:
Pain follows close on pleasure.

Slow tread the winding measure
Yet it is swiftly done,
The summer spills her treasure:
Pain follows close on pleasure.

Ian Warren 1917 -

Down by the Salley Gardens

Down by the salley gardens my love and I did meet;
She passed the salley gardens with little snow-white feet.
She bid me take love easy, as the leaves grow on the tree;
But I, being young and foolish, with her would not agree.

In a field by the river my love and I did stand,
And on my leaning shoulder she laid her snow-white hand.
She bid me take life easy, as the grass grows on the weirs;
But I was young and foolish, and now am full of tears.

William Butler Yeats 1865 – 1939

He wishes for the Cloths of Heaven

Had I the heaven's embroidered cloths,
Enwrought with golden and silver light,
The blue and the dim and the dark cloths
Of night and light and the half-light,
I would spread the cloths under your feet:
But I, being poor, have only my dreams;
I have spread my dreams under your feet;
Tread softly because you tread on my dreams.

William Butler Yeats

The Wild Swans at Coole

The trees are in their autumn beauty,
The woodland paths are dry
Under the October twilight the water
Mirrors a still sky;
Upon the brimming water among the stones
Are nine-and-fifty swans.

The nineteenth autumn has come upon me
Since I first made my count;
I saw, before I had well finished,
All suddenly mount
And scatter wheeling in great broken rings
Upon their clamorous wings.

I have looked upon those brilliant creatures,
And now my heart is sore.
All's changed since I, hearing at twilight,
The first time on this shore,
The bell-beat of their wings above my head,
Trod with a lighter tread.

Unwearied still, lover by lover,
They paddle in the cold
Companionable streams or climb the air;
Their hearts have not grown old;
Passion or conquest, wander where they will,
Attend upon them still.

But now they drift on the still water,
Mysterious, beautiful;
Among what rushes will they build,
By what lake's edge or pool
Delight men's eyes when I awake some day
To find they have flown away?

William Butler Yeats

The Song of Wandering Aengus

I went out to the hazel wood,
Because a fire was in my head,
And cut and peeled a hazel wand,
And hooked a berry to a thread;
And when white moths were on the wing,
And moth-like stars were flickering out,
I dropped the berry in a stream
And caught a little silver trout.

When I had laid it on the floor
I went to blow the fire aflame,
But something rustled on the floor,
And some one called me by my name:
It had become a glimmering girl
With apple blossom in her hair
Who called me by my name and ran
And faded through the brightening air.

Though I am old with wandering
Through hollow lands and hilly lands,
I will find out where she has gone,
And kiss her lips and take her hands;
And walk among long dappled grass,
And pluck till time and times are done
The silver apples of the moon,
The golden apples of the sun.

William Butler Yeats

The Lake Isle of Innisfree

I will arise and go now, and go to Innisfree,
And a small cabin build there, of clay and wattles made:
Nine bean-rows will I have there, a hive for the honey-bee,
And live alone in the bee-loud glade.

And I shall have some peace there,
for peace comes dropping slow,
Dropping from the veils of the morning to where the cricket
sings;
There midnight's all a glimmer, and noon a purple glow,
And evening full of the linnet's wings.

I will arise and go now, for always night and day
I hear lake water lapping with low sounds by the shore;
While I standing on the roadway, or on the pavements grey,
I hear it in the deep heart's core.

William Butler Yeats

When You are Old

When you are old and grey and full of sleep,
And nodding by the fire, take down this book,
And slowly read, and dream of the soft look
Your eyes had once, and their shadows deep;

How many loved your moments of glad grace,
And loved your beauty with love false or true,
But one man loved the pilgrim soul in you,
And loved the sorrows of your changing face;

And bending down beside the glowing bars,
Murmur, a little sadly, how Love fled
And paced upon the mountains overhead
And hid his face amid a crowd of stars.

William Butler Yeats